ASHLEY JONDLE

RESTORATION

Words of hope as you **JOURNAL** toward healing

RESTORATION

Restoration –Copyright ©2025 by Ashley Jondle

Published by UNITED HOUSE Publishing

All rights reserved. No portion of this book may be reproduced or shared in any form–electronic, printed, photocopied, recording, or by any information storage and retrieval system, without prior written permission from the publisher. The use of short quotations is permitted.

Scriptures taken from the Holy Bible, New International Version®, NIV®. Copyright ©1973, 1978, 1984, 2011 by Biblica, Inc.™ Used by permission of Zondervan. All rights reserved worldwide. www.zondervan.com The "NIV" and "New International Version" are trademarks registered in the United States Patent and Trademark Office by Biblica, Inc.™

The Holy Bible, English Standard Version® (ESV®) © 2001 by Crossway, a publishing ministry of Good News Publishers.
All rights reserved.

ISBN: 978-1-952840-69-2

UNITED HOUSE Publishing
Waterford, Michigan

info@unitedhousepublishing.com
www.unitedhousepublishing.com

Cover Layout and Interior Design:
Talitha McGuinness; talitha@unitedhousepublishing.com

Printed in the United States of America
2025–First Edition
SPECIAL SALES
Most UNITED HOUSE books are available at special quantity discounts when purchased in bulk by corporations, organizations, and special-interest groups. For information, please e-mail orders@unitedhousepublishing.com.

Contents

Welcome

Laying The Groundwork

Insecurities Don't Define Me

The Fighting Season

Restoration

RESTORATION

Welcome

Hey friend,

    I am excited for you to begin to see God's hand of restoration in your life as you journal your way toward healing.

    There is healing to be found in putting pen to paper. There is healing in working through your struggles, doubts, and insecurities. There is healing in surrendering it all to God and trusting Him to do what only He can do.

    As you go through this journal, write your own story. Know you are not alone as you walk through feelings of loneliness and times of questioning.

    I pray this journal brings encouragement to your heart, knowing restoration is not only possible, but it's happening now through the struggles and the pain. Nothing is impossible for God. Allow His Word to sustain you in this season and bring light to a dark time.

RESTORATION

RESTORATION

Laying the Groundwork

RESTORATION

Laying the Groundwork

I never thought I would get to this place in my life: truly happy, loved, and with an overall sense of wholeness. As I sit here writing this, though, I remember all too well the excruciating pain life brought just years before.

At eighteen, I knew it all, or so I thought. I didn't like being told what I could or couldn't do, especially when it came to whom I thought was my "one true love." If only I knew then what I know now, I would have realized how terribly wrong I was. I could have altered the path my life was on and ultimately had a really different story.

Let me start back at the beginning. At eighteen years old, I left home and lived with friends. It didn't go as I had planned, and just two weeks before graduating high school, I found myself homeless. I dropped out of school and moved to Illinois with my boyfriend.

I was a Christian girl, raised in a Christian home, walking down a road I never thought I'd travel. My sin and pride had taken over, and my shame and regret made me feel unforgivable. I had gone from the youth music leader to living in sin with my boyfriend. I knew it was wrong, but because my shame held me captive, I decided to marry my boyfriend in hopes that by doing so, I would free my conscience from the life I was living.

Everything continued to fall apart. I learned after marrying my husband that he was partaking

RESTORATION

in things that were not honoring God's design of marriage. Instead of accepting God's grace, I pridefully kept to myself, hoping I could fix my husband.

It took moving to three different states and becoming pregnant with my first child to realize my efforts were of no good. I couldn't fix my husband, at least not on my own. In a desperate attempt to put my life back together, I cried out to God asking for forgiveness. I knew I had messed up, and it wasn't anyone's fault but my own. I also knew I had chosen this marriage. Despite the impossibility my marriage presented, I asked God to restore it. I knew I needed help.

As time went on, it was clear my marriage wasn't getting any better, yet God began working within me, teaching me to trust Him as He restored and refined me. I realized I needed to stop worrying about my husband, and I needed to put focus into improving myself and building my own personal relationship with Christ.

I wholeheartedly believed in restoration, but I knew it could only come when I put my pride aside and gave grace and forgiveness where it was not deserved or even earned.

I focused on loving my husband. I prayed for him, myself, and our marriage regularly, giving the hard times to God.

> "Let us then approach God's throne of grace with confidence, so that we may receive mercy and find grace to help us in our time of need."
> Hebrews 4:16, NIV

God hears our prayers and wants our requests, thanksgiving, and praises to be brought before Him. List your prayer requests in the space provided.

RESTORATION

Nine months later, I gave birth to our first son. I gave my attention to being the best mama I could be for him, despite my husband's absence. The things I experienced were painful and life shattering, and I cried out to God, asking "Why?" It didn't feel like the most appropriate response, as I know I brought it on myself by being in a toxic relationship from the very start, but I was hurting.

I fought for my marriage and I fought for my husband. Don't be mistaken, I was far from the perfect wife and didn't always handle every situation as I should have. As I was fighting *for* my husband, I would often find myself fighting *with* my husband.

I persevered, staying in the marriage day in and day out, and we eventually had two more pregnancies resulting in miscarriages. This was one of the hardest things I had to go through because, despite being married, I felt completely alone.

I experienced so much self-disapproval and anger. As my husband drew further away from me, I wondered what I was doing wrong, always questioning why I wasn't enough. Was I not pretty enough? Not good enough? Not smart enough? I was always thinking, "There must be something wrong with *me*."

You might find yourself in a similar position, questioning your worth. There are so many voices that want to come in and drown out the truth of who God says we are. How is what you're walking through, impacting what you believe about yourself? Take some time to journal this.

_____
_____
_____
_____
_____
_____
_____
_____
_____

My insecurities stemmed from what I went through. It's taken a long time to reshape my thoughts and ultimately my heart. Sometimes I find myself believing the lies I'd been told, but as I open the Word, I am reminded of who God says I am.

RESTORATION

I am loved. Loved by a God who created me in my mother's womb, fully knowing me, yet He still chose me (Jeremiah 1:15). Despite what I may go through, I know I am not alone. He said, "Never will I leave you; never will I forsake you" (Hebrews 13:5 NIV). The peace within me need not waver as I go through difficult situations and experience hardships.

What are some verses that remind you of God's faithfulness? These truths don't change based on your circumstances. God is good, even when it doesn't feel like it. It's easier to believe in His faithfulness in the midst of despair, when you can look back and see His character of faithfulness revealed over and over again in your life. Jot down these verses for future reference.

As you may find yourself being tempted to fall back into despair, remember that God is for you and knows what is ahead of you.

_____

_____

_____

_____

_____

_____

_____

_____

_____

RESTORATION

"'For I know the plans I have for you,' declares the Lord, 'plans to prosper you and not to harm you, plans to give you hope and a future.'"
Jeremiah 29:11, NIV

Insecurities Don't Define Me

RESTORATION

RESTORATION

Insecurities Don't Define Me

As women, we have an internal need to feel loved. When we don't feel loved, our whole sense of identity seems to be shattered.

"Husbands, love your wives, just as Christ loved the church and gave himself up for her."
Ephesians 5:25, NIV

Husbands are instructed to *love* their wives. Without love, especially from your husband, insecurities find a way to sneak into your heart. Not having the love of my husband caused me to doubt myself and my self-worth. Having grown up in the church, I knew Christ loved me, but none of that seemed to matter when my earthly relationship clouded my spiritual knowledge.

But that's just it. God's love for me couldn't just be spiritual knowledge; it needed to seep into my heart and the very being of who I was. My identity needed to be rooted in Christ, who He is, and what He says of me. Only then could I stand firm in truth, despite the walls crumbling down around me. Only then could I find stability and peace. My identity should not change due to the circumstances happening all around me, but my identity should be anchored to Christ's love.

The more I reached out to Jesus and got into His word, the more at peace I was. My circumstances had not changed, and my marriage was not better.

RESTORATION

But instead of relying on myself, I found strength and joy in who God was and always will be.

Reflect on a time when you found strength in God despite how impossible your circumstances may have seemed.

_____
_____
_____
_____
_____
_____
_____
_____
_____
_____
_____

"The steadfast love of the Lord never ceases; His mercies never come to an end; they are new every morning; great is your faithfulness."
Lamentations 3:22-23, ESV

God is good! Once I truly believed in my heart that God was and is forever good, my identity found rest in Him.

RESTORATION

"Give thanks to the Lord for He is good;
his love endures forever."
Psalm 107:1, NIV

I went from saying "Am I enough?" to "Who does God say I am?" As those questions began to shift, so did my mindset. I focused my mind on Godly things, and my heart followed.

"Set your mind on things above, not on earthly things."
Colossians 3:2, NIV

When you know and believe your identity is found in Christ, everything changes. You first need to identify the lies you are believing about yourself and recognize who you've allowed to speak into your life. Only then can you surrender it all to Christ, allowing Him to cleanse and renew.

Write down lies you have found yourself believing, and next to them, find some verses that remind you of your true identity in Christ. As you journal these lies vs. truths, be reminded of His steadfast and unconditional love. Allow His Words to speak louder than the lies you've been believing.

_____

_____

_____

_____

_____

_____

RESTORATION

I am not who my husband says I am.
I am not who I often find myself believing I am.
I am a child of God.
I am loved.
I am His.
That is my identity.

    As I began to let that truth marinate, it didn't matter anymore that my husband didn't love me. Sometimes I would find myself sitting in a pool of despair and soaking in my feelings of rejection and loneliness, but just as quickly as those negative thoughts came, I would find comfort in Christ.

    Rejection and loneliness had the power to destroy me and bury me alive, but I took that power back and rested my life in the hands of Jesus, knowing He would never let me go.

    Rejection and loneliness don't have the final say. Take your thoughts captive when they appear, desiring to steal your joy.

    Write about a time when you found supernatural peace and joy in Christ, in the middle of great sadness.

_____
_____
_____
_____
_____
_____

RESTORATION

As you walk through a season of suffering, be reminded that God is always with you. He will turn your sorrow into joy for His glory and in His time.

*"The Lord himself goes before you
and will be with you;
he will never leave you nor forsake you.
Do not be afraid; do not be discouraged."*
Deuteronomy 31:8, NIV

RESTORATION

RESTORATION

The Fighting Season

RESTORATION

RESTORATION

The Fighting Season

Once I was able to understand my insecurities and how God's love for me could completely alter my beliefs about myself, I was able to love the way I should have all along. I could love without any expectation or desire for something in return. With this new way of loving, I entered into the fighting season.

Fighting was easy. The real challenge was going from fighting with my husband, to fighting for my husband. I had become really good at fighting *with* him and needed no help in that department. It was learning how to fight *for* my husband that I sought counsel.

One of the most important ideas I was repeatedly told was that when fighting *for* my husband, I needed to have boundaries. Boundaries to protect my health and my heart.

My husband had lost my trust and acted in ways that made it unsafe to partake in the sexual intimacy that should be enjoyed between a husband and wife. But in order to reach my husband on a deeper, emotional level and in order to protect my own body, I needed to abstain from anything that could potentially be dangerous or harmful.

Having boundaries and sticking with those boundaries made the marriage relationship difficult—as if it wasn't difficult enough already. My husband thought these boundaries were unfair, and instead of having open eyes and an open heart to his own mistakes, he used this as an excuse to point blame.

RESTORATION

His words hurt. I was at a loss and I didn't know what to do. I was fighting for my marriage and had safely created boundaries, but it only seemed to make my husband even more upset, and pull further and further away from me.

Every day it became harder and harder to fight *for* my husband. Despite my best attempts, I would end up fighting *with* him.

Allowing the hurt to consume me and reacting harshly didn't provide true relief from my pain, but I tricked myself into believing it made me feel a little better. And maybe it did in the moment. But at the end of the day I was still hurt, broken, and searching for God. God seemed gone, or at least distant. I knew He cared about what I was going through, but why was restoration not happening? I had spent many nights on my knees. I had given my situation to God, yet my husband still hadn't changed. In fact, it seemed to have gotten even worse.

Every self-help book I'd read told me about restoration and God's ability to save a broken marriage, but God wasn't saving my marriage, and I wondered why. Was there something I could have done differently?

You may be in a place where you, too, feel as if you are all alone. You may be wondering if God even hears you when you are calling out for an answer to prayer.

Do you find yourself doubting God's ability to restore because your circumstances aren't changing the way you had hoped and believed? Reflect here in the space provided.

RESTORATION

_____

Doubt will come, but it doesn't have to stay. Write a prayer asking God to help you have faith, even when you haven't yet seen an answer to your prayer. Believe He is able to do the impossible and wait on His answer expectantly.

_____

RESTORATION

"In the morning, Lord, you hear my voice; in the morning I lay my requests before you and wait expectantly."
Psalm 5:3, NIV

Looking back, I know I did all I could to fight for my marriage. I do not regret believing, nor do I doubt for a minute that God can and does in fact save marriages. He didn't save mine, and although it hurt in the moment, God had a plan for my life that would far exceed any dream I could have imagined. Choosing to go through with my divorce was one of the hardest choices I have ever made. It took letting go of what I thought my life was going to look like and accepting that God wanted to create something beautiful out of the broken pieces of the choices I'd made.

What I know now, is that God *does* restore. Not in the way I had spent years praying for, but in a totally unexpected, miraculous way that I am forever grateful for.

RESTORATION

Restoration

RESTORATION

Restoration

I thought I knew what restoration was. I believed that it was God restoring my marriage. It was my husband becoming a man of God, changing his ways, and loving his family. I was deceived into believing that if those things didn't happen, restoration wasn't for me.

I didn't realize I was believing a lie from the pit of hell. There isn't a single part of what I've walked through that has left me broken beyond repair. There is freedom in understanding that restoration doesn't always look like life going as you had hoped and planned. Restoration may be God using all of the broken pieces that you have surrendered to create something beautiful.

Let go of the need to control your story and trust that God, in His sovereignty, will redeem it for His Glory.

In what ways do you need to surrender to His plan in your life, trusting that He can make all things new? Write them down here.

_____

_____

_____

_____

RESTORATION

"Behold, I am doing a new thing; now it springs forth, do you not perceive it? I will make a way in the wilderness and rivers in the desert."
Isaiah 43:19, ESV

Allow Jesus to do what only He can do and trust Him as He works. He's really good at taking nothing and making something beautiful.

Write a prayer below asking God to help you surrender your own ideas and submit to His plans for your life.

_____
_____
_____
_____
_____
_____
_____

When God restores, He does so in abundance. He doesn't just return something to its original condition, but He makes it better than it ever was. Let's look at Job. This man had lost everything, but through it all he remained fixed on the Lord. When God restored, He did so in abundance, giving Job twice as much as he had previously (Job 42:10).

Not only did Jesus bring restoration to my family by providing the most loving husband, but He restored my inner self. There is no longer a meaningless and painful emptiness at the core of who I am. There is so much hope and life as Jesus consumes every part of my being. He took the brokenness of my own actions and created something beautiful.

I look back in awe of who He is and I can see His hand at work in my life. I pray the same for you. I pray as you journal through the hardship, you can more clearly see God's goodness in all things. Know that you are not alone. He sees you. He hears you. As you are transformed more into the image of Jesus, He is restoring you, bringing the ultimate freedom.

Use the space below to thank God for who He is and what He is doing in your life. Seasons come and go, feelings may waver, but God is the same through it all and He is worthy of our praise.

_____

_____

_____

_____

_____

_____

"Search me, O God, and know my heart! Try me and know my thoughts! And see if there be any grievous way in me, and lead me in the way everlasting!"
Psalm 139:23-24, ESV

RESTORATION

RESTORATION

Ashley Jondle is a devoted wife and mother of seven, living in Missouri on 10 acres of land.

Her own story of restoration has given her a heart for women experiencing difficulties in their own lives. Currently pursuing a Lay Biblical Counseling certificate, Ashley is committed to equipping herself with the tools to counsel others while always pointing them to the hope of Jesus. Ashley loves studying the Word of God, spending time with her family, and enjoying a hot cup of coffee.

www.ingramcontent.com/pod-product-compliance
Lightning Source LLC
Chambersburg PA
CBHW062055280426
43673CB00073B/132